UHIBBU'ALLAH: I LOVE ALLAH

QUEST FOR FAITH WHILST YOU TRAVERSE LIFE

ALIYA ZACKRIA

For those who see themselves in **Jannah**

whilst taking tiny steps right from this **Dunya**

Contents

Contents

Contents

Preface

We as muslims are travellers from this world to the hereafter, our stay is short in this temporary life to what Allah  promised for us in eternity. Our lives are no less than a challenge to find faith, even though we grow up in muslim families, finding faith has always been a personal journey and oh what a beautiful journey! What have you tasted in this world if you haven't tasted the sweetness of emaan?! Our parents never force Islamic laws on us but they only introduce and no doubt they're not just laws but a way of life and we love to follow them, Islam is a way of life, the road to peace and eternal happiness.

In this book, you will see how I have found myself the deep love for Allah . Each phase of my life has helped me to find that connection with Allah and I want to share that journey with all the readers because I know we all go through the same feelings, thoughts and emotions at some point in life. I am not perfect in my deen, the more I learn; the more I realize how little I know. There is always **quest**to learn more, be more and do more for Allah. This book features a curated collection of fifty poems and I hope you could relate to these poems. As you turn the pages, I pray you find a deeper and more beautiful love for Allah, see my perception of faith and how I envision this bond with Allah. I pray our hearts are never void of love. I pray Allah fills our hearts with His love.

Acknowledgements

I am forever thankful to Allah  for His divine guidance and love which helped me to complete this book. I want to thank my loved ones who inspired, supported and guided me throughout the process of writing this book. I would also like to extend my special gratitude to an individual whose thoughful suggestions greatly contributed to shaping the title of this book.

Prologue

May you find ease for your troubled mind,
May you find tranquility for your lost soul,
May you find love for your empty heart,
May these poems bring back your spark.
Turn the pages, let Allah's  love descend,
One rhyme at a time, gentle on your heart,
Each poem tells a story close to my heart,
These are not just poems, they are an art.

Introduction

Assalamualaikum warahmatullahi wabarkatuhu
May the peace, mercy and blessings of Allah ﷻ be upon you

Dear reader, didn't you buy this book because you love Allah? ﷻ Now you've taken your first step, now wait; let Allah ﷻ get closer to you as you turn the pages. Each page is a love story from a soul who wants to imbibe the love of Allah ﷻ in the hearts of others. Each poem is penned down for you to reflect and draw closer to Allah ﷻ. This has not come down in a form of poetry within days, it's from a soul who has gathered all their experiences and knowledge then turned it into beautiful poetry for readers. All praise is for Allah ﷻ who guided me and made it possible for me.

I pray every soul who is looking for love, finds Allah's ﷻ love first and foremost. I pray every disturbed mind and shattered heart goes to Allah ﷻ before seeking solution anywhere else. You might not have all the answers to your questoning mind and empty heart but with Allah ﷻ tranquility descends like the rain in the desert. Dear reader, I hope when you reach the last page, your heart is filled with Allah's ﷻ love. As Allah ﷻ says "Whoever comes to Me walking, I will come to him running."-Sahih Al Bukhari 7405. Life is certainly not easy but remember if you have Allah's ﷻ love, no matter what you go through, Allah's ﷻ love shall pave a way of miracles for you. My favourite quote is "If you've got Allah's ﷻ love, you've got everything you need," so let's begin, Bismillah.

1. CHOSEN ONE

She knows she is the chosen one,

Cause Allah  chose her to be the one.

He said; He tests only those He loves,

And she knows she is loved.

The tests she had; trembled her spirit,

But hey! It can also be a Jannah ticket.

2. PLANS

Oh Allah , my plans may be good with my limited knowledge,
But Ya Rabb, Your plans are best for me as You are The All knowing.
While my decisions may harm me in the near future,
Yours will only protect me and keep me happy forever.

3. DECEPTION

I thought life was so bright,
And I used to just delight.
Looking back; I was impressed by fame,
If I think today; I find it so lame.
I used to run behind success,
But I forgot the ultimate source of success.
Friends, I thought they would be forever,
But they just treated me like "whatever".
Crying, I used to spend all my nights,
Unless I found the ultimate light.
I found the path of deen,
And today it makes me feel like a queen.
Today, I might just be an unknown,
But I hope, in Allah's sight I'm known.

4. TRIALS I

Dear heart,

It's okay to walk through tribulations;

If Jannah and Allah's  love are your destinations.

❧❧❧

5. TRIALS II

Every time a calamity hits,
Making you shriek, shiver and grit,
Remember Allah  is by your side,
Neither Has He left you alone nor denied,
Soon the storms will transcend,
Your blessings will ascend,
Sabr runs in us so we never complain,
Just like the new morning and the new moon,
Indeed, all your worries will end soon,
Meanwhile, all we say is "Inna lillahi wa inna ilaihi rajioon."

6. TRIALS III

Give glad tidings to the believers for they are warriors,
Even if they lose everything here, in Jannah they are scorers.
Trials will come and shake your spirit,
Hold tight to your deen, you'll be given without limit.
You're rewarded even for the thorn that pricks,
Allah  keeps all records, expect full reward for all your hardships.

7. HARDSHIP & EASE I

• 7 •

The author of the Qur'ān said "with hardship comes ease."
I'm rest assured there's relief even in my pain,
Goodness even in my struggles and benefit even in all my losses.
I trust you completely with all my affairs Allah .
"Indeed, there is ease with hardship.
Most certainly, there is ease with hardship." Al Qur'ān 94:5-6

8. HARDSHIP & EASE II

• 8 •

If you ever feel like giving up in this world,
Remember Allah ﷻ and His word,
"With hardships comes ease,"
This moment too will pass like a breeze.
Solid faith in Allah ﷻ will carry you through,
It's the promise of Allah ﷻ and it's true!

9. HARDSHIP & EASE III

When Allah  said "With hardship comes ease" remember,
This world can be the 'hardship' and Jannah the 'ease.'
Let your struggles help you level up in Jannah.
The more hardships, the higher the reward.
Earn a lot of Jannah points, so that Allah ﷻ can appoint
You in the highest ranks of Jannah.

10. RESISTANCE I

When the sin lures us and when our desires call us,

May our soul resist the urge and be aware of Allah's  presence.

"Does he not know that Allah is watching?" -Al Qur'ān 96:14

11. RESISTANCE II

Given a chance to stand in front of Allah ﷻ
And commit the sin, we will NEVER,
Yet our innocent mind thinks Allah ﷻ
Isn't watching when we sin. How ironic!
Yet Al'Ghafur, The Ever Forgiving,
Forgives you like you never committed
In the first place...How Magnificent!

12. ISTIGHFAR I

Seek Allah's  forgiveness; do ample of Istighfar,
Come back to Him, even if you have gone too far.
Your Lord; not only forgives your sins but also erases,
This is from His grace and to Him belongs all praises.

13. ISTIGHFAR II

Allah  said, "True repentance done from your heart,
Indeed, turns all your sins into rewards."
This is how beautiful is our islam,
That's why we admire its charm.

14. ISTIGHFAR III

Allah  will never punish you; if you truly seek forgiveness,
A drop of tear you shed is more beloved to Him than Ocean waters.
Never lose hope in Him, never lose trust in Him,
He is forgiving and merciful, The Ghafoorur Raheem.

15. ENVELOPED

Souls that stand before Allah  are covered by His protection,
Enveloped in His love and flooded by His blessings.
Keep Allah close to keep your happiness closer and everlasting.

16. EMAAN

Emaan and good deeds (amaal-e-saleh) go hand in hand.
It's impossible for a believer to have faith and
Not do good deeds or do good deeds without having faith.

17. FOUNTAIN OF EMAAN

Blessed are those who find Allah ﷻ in young age,

Blessed are those who attach themselves to houses of Allah ﷻ,

Blessed are the believers who consider the laws of Allah ﷻ,

Blessed are those who stand before Allah ﷻ five times a day,

Blessed are those who cannot go a day without conversing

With Allah ﷻ through Qur'ān, indeed blessed are those in

Whose heart is the fountain of emaan.

18. TAHAJJUD

You cry and ask,

He will smile and give.

How will He not when you meet Him in the most loved time,

When He descends to the lowest heaven just for His few special ones.

19. DU'Ā AT TAHAJJUD

Out of everything you could ever possibly do during night,
Your heart desired His presence.
He comes down to the lowest heaven just to hear you call out Him.
O what a beautiful meeting, just you and Him,
Covered in the darkness of night.
You being the slave and He the king,
Wanting to say "kun" (Be) for your every beautiful dream.

20. SALAH I

If Allah  has given you the opportunity to bow down,
You're amongst a blessed few, who're crowned.
To have this level of emaan is so precious,
Your Lord chose you, Who's Most Gracious.

21. SALAH II

If they ask "What keeps you strong?"

Tell them "It's the love of Allah ﷻ."

If they ask "How are you certain of Allah's ﷻ love?"

Tell them "He calls me five times a day,

Just to fulfill all of my needs,

With His love being my top most need.

He doesn't lose anything with my sujood

But I gain everything with my sujood.

A love that knows to give and give."

22. JUMMAH

Every Friday, I pray all your du'as are answered,

May Allah hear your every desire which this world unheard.

Tidy yourself and get ready for Jummah,

This is not a trend, but it's a sunnah.

"This is the best day of the week", said by our RasoolAllah ﷺ,

Also on Jummah; do send ample salams to our RasoolAllah ﷺ.

Consider it as Eid; avoid fasting on Friday except in

Ramadan, Ashura, Arafah and White Days.

On friday, Adam AS was created, sent to earth,

On friday, his repentance was accepted, he was sent to paradise.

A surah in Qur'ān is named after Jummah, also

Safety from grave trials is given to those who pass away on Jummah.

On Friday, Qayamah is said to occur,

Do more good deeds, as on Friday to Allah they are more dearer.

This is the day which has an hour in which du'ās are accepted,

Don't forget to read surah Kahf for it holds great virtues and reward.

23. QIYAM AL LAYL

There's beauty in night and darkness,

You can't see the light except when it's dark,

You never know, perhaps your Du'ās glow brighter than

The moon when they're travelling all the way up to Allah ﷻ.

That's why Allah ﷻ chose nights, even the smallest spark of

Night glows so much bright and there's blessing over daylight,

So go bow down to your Lord and ask for every delight,

The night is long and your Lord is The Most Generous and Might.

24. IBADAH OF HEART

Reward me for every desire I give up for your sake Allah ,
Let my heart know that there is a next stop; the aakhirah.
Keep my heart grounded by your aqeedah,
May my heart always be in your ibadah!

25. RAMADAN

O Ramadan, please tell me your secret,
How is that everyone becomes so perfect?
Everyone tries their very best,
Like it's their last test.
The nights are so beautiful
And days are so blissful
O Ramadan, I fear you'll take away
All the good deeds with you,
How can I be assured that I'll continue
Evenafter it's without you ?
O Ramadan, make my imaan so strong
Even if you go, I hope I will never go wrong.

26. QADR OF ALLAH ﷻ

Please don't tell you you've tried everything
Until you've spoken to your Lord at midnight.
Your hard work is incomplete without
You speaking to Him about it.
He's the one who grants,
He's the key to every door of your life,
He is the one who blesses and
He's the one to block something out of your life.
Be rest assured whatever He does, it's for your best.

27. SAKE OF ALLAH 

Take care of other's hearts and

Allah ﷻ will take care of your heart.

Nothing done for the sake of Allah ﷻ

Goes unnoticed, it's surely a rewarding act!

28. PUT ALLAH  FIRST

Paths become beautiful when you have Allah ﷻ by your side,

You put Allah ﷻ first and suddenly everything seems so light.

Set your priorities straight, let them be aakhirah focused,

Let deen be your compass and in return Allah will keep you blessed.

Detach yourself from anything that takes you away from Allah,

Follow His guidance and you will never be lost, Bi'iznillah.

29. ALLAH  STAYS

Who stayed?

"Allah."

Oh, forever?

"Yes, forever!"

"He is with you wherever you are." Al Qur'ān 57:4

❧❧❧

30. HAVING ALLAH 

Those who have no one; have Allah ﷻ,

Those who have His friendship;

Have the greatest companionship,

Those who look for hope; He becomes The light.

Those who have lost themselves; He guides them.

He never lets down His servants.

He is sufficient for all your affairs and

He causes miracles for those who trust Him.

He will heal you, enrich you, sustain you and

Love you like no other, for He is your Allah ﷻ.

31. RELY ON ALLAH 

Ya Rabbi, never leave my hand,
For when the world turns their back,
I know You are the only One I can rely On.

32. ALLAH'S  SLAVE

I told Allah ﷻ, "My heart is broken,"
He replied "I am The Repairer and The Restorer (Al-Jabbar)"
I told Him "I'm weak and fragile,"
He replied "I am strong (Al-Qawiyy)."
I told Him "I am feeling disturbed,"
He replied "I'm The Owner of peace (As-Salam)."
You can always find bits and pieces of Allah's ﷻ love in you,
No matter how far you stray away from Him,
Because at the end of the day you belong to Him.
You're Allah's ﷻ slave. Allah ﷻ will take care of you.

33. ALLAH  AS FRIEND

O Allah, keep my heart in your tender care,
This world is too rude and causes my eyes to tear,
Don't let me be alone, You be my friend,
Yours is the only love which has no end.

34. ALLAH'S جَلَّ جَلَالُه PRESENCE

Little did she know that her Lord is in full control of her.
She would be completely broken and
Her Lord would heal her all over again,
She would not know where she was walking and
Her Lord would guide her, she would trip and
Fall but her Lord would catch her.
Sometimes she thinks she is lonely but
Her Lord lets her know His presence.
She called out to Allah جَلَّ جَلَالُه and He was there for her.

35. ALLAH ﷻ RESPONDS

You've continuously heard me and my wants,

And every time, I'm just in awe of Your response!

You've given me the world's best of the best,

I'm blessed to have kept my heart at your crest.

Every time I doubted Your rejections,

Silly me! It was only for my protection.

Keep me steadfast on Your path

And protect me from Your wrath.

Oh how Merciful, The extremely Merciful!

I absolutely love being different for your sake,

Definitely want to win aakhirah at duniya's stake.

You've already told, the greater; the faith, the harder; the trials.

My Lord, I also know, the tougher; the trials, the greater; the reward.

I love being chosen by You, Please choose me for Jannah too,

Just our love, me and You. More than Jannah, it was always ABOUT
YOU!

36. AL'QUR'ĀN

There isn't any book which has ever been this close to my heart,
Perhaps cause I feel so close to it when all else departs.
More than a book, its a companion, a friend;
You'll be shocked to see how its words can mend.
The only book which can intercede till the times of end,
Please while you're still alive, don't forget to befriend!
Do give it a read, even a single verse, make it the habit of your days,
So you'd feel safe when in front of your eyes, your life replays!
The stories of the Prophets will give you so much courage,
Trust me, after every letter you recite you'll feel so much encouraged.
It speaks directly to you as you want it to be spoken,
Mending every part and bit of you if it was ever broken.
It has in it, a love full of ocean;
Giving reason to every confusing emotion.
This is a book called Al'Qur'ān,
Given through the most honest man.

If it wasn't for Allah's  love for us, We wouldn't have had it.

Make it the compass of your life and make sure you treasure it.

Don't let it be abandoned on the shelf,

Cause it's for your heart and for your self.

The heaven and earth has already heard it's praises,

Now it's your turn to recite and check how much your Emaan rises.

For Allah ﷻ Himself says about Qur'ān in Qur'ān:

That "This is the book, in it is guidance" (2:2),

So give importance to it as it is Jannah's license.

That "This is a book which We have revealed as a blessing" (6:155)

So stop your thoughts of doubt and second guessing.

That "We have revealed for you (O men) a book in which

there is a message for you, will you then not understand?" (21:10)

Yet we open all other messages, in hurry and curiosity still

never bothered to see what message Allah ﷻ has sent!

37. SABR

I have witnessed many battles in my life,
I knew what befell upon me; I could handle it in my life.
I know You said; You do not burden a soul beyond it can bear,
Come what may I know You are always there.
A prick of a thorn in life or any setback,
Ya Rabb, I know You will always have my back!

38. SHUKR

Oh Allah, I'm so grateful for every blessing,
This is Your rehma that you keep giving.
You gave me everything my heart desired,
My Rabb, Your praises are always exalted!
Alhamdulillah, for all the blessings that I receive without measure,
I've witnessed myself, You give more with every thankful gesture;
"If you're grateful, I will surely give you more and more." Al Qur'ān
14:7

39. DHIKR

Surely in the remembrance of Allah  do hearts find rest,
There's uniqueness about dhikr; Qur'ān; salah, that makes us best.
Heart enters into tranquility and all the chaos fade,
Surely, Allah eases every task after it is prayed.

40. QALB

Hearts are fragile so hand it over to Allah ﷻ ,
He is the Creator, He will guard it from every flaw,
A precious spot should be given to chosen and blessed ones,
First Allah ﷻ, then RasoolAllah ﷺ then Allah's ﷻ creation comes.

41. SADAQAH

If you have the opportunity, give ample charity,
Every penny will return to you in prosperity.
Spend in Allah's  way, without thinking twice,
It's guaranteed to return you multiplied many times.
So invest in your aakhirah's account,
Allah ﷻ will give you in both worlds without account.

42. SALAM

The one to initiate salam is the one closest to Allah  ,
So let go of grudges and smile at people for the sake of Allah ,
Remember Allah loves the doers of good,
Be a bigger person, for Allah you should!

43. BLESSINGS

Being happy for others in their blessings is a mark of solid emaan,
It's only because you know who the provider is, "Ya Rehman."
You never cringe, compare or feel jealous of anyone's blessings,
Cause you're sure, He will give you ample when it's your timing.
So you see and send du'ās to others when they are happy,
Trust your Lord, He will never let your hands be empty.

44. FAMILY ON DEEN

A family on deen is a legacy to leave behind,

What an honour it is to have your faith aligned,

Be mindful of Allah  in all your relationships,

Hold tight to your deen with all your grip,

Your legacy is the deen you imbibe in the hearts of others,

And in the aakhirah; your deen on the scales is what truly matters.

45. OBEY ALLAH ﷻ & HIS MESSENGER ﷺ

When there are two paths to be chosen,

Between the right and lonely,

And the wrong and solidarity,

Find the path of Allah ﷻ because we not only say

" La ilaha illallah muhammadur RasoolAllah ﷺ,"

We also abide by it by,

"Wa ati'ullaha wa ati'ur'Rasool ﷺ."

46. RASOOLALLAH ﷺ

Not a single picture of RasoolAllah  exists,
Yet his teachings are precious to us as gifts.
He was chosen for Qur'ān and sunnah,
Let's follow every step of his as an Ummah.

47. JANNAH I

We keep sinning; You always keep forgiving,
Many reminders we get, yet we forget You keep recording,
Ya Rabb; Sometimes our desires aren't in our control,
Keep our hearts firm so that we achieve Jannah; our goal!

48. JANNAH II

What's so special about Jannah?
In Jannah we will see Allah ,
In Jannah we will meet RasoolAllah ﷺ,
In Jannah there is no separation,
In Jannah happiness is eternal.

49. JANNATI

Residents of Jannah; are the believers,

They're the ones, who were strivers.

They abode in the highest ranks of Jannah,

As well as they are wrapped in Allah's  love and rehma.

Their thirst is quenched with the rivers of wine, honey and milk,

They adorn themselves in the garments of jannah's purest silk.

Their soul feels calm with Jannah's breeze,

Their soul stays with Allah in bliss and peace.

50. VIEW OF JANNAH

The Place, that's filled with love,

Where the heart would find peace,

Where no one breaks the heart of one another,

All they want to see is happiness in each other.

The place, no human has ever been;

The place, that no eye has ever seen.

I'm running short of words to describe it because of its awe.

There are Rivers of honey, milk and wine.

The sand of musk, the breeze of loyalty, trust and faith.

Dresses? Beautiful gowns of fine and purest silk.

The place where your eyes ain't gonna be any ordinary eyes

For your eyes will view the King Of All Kings

When He unveils Himself, subhanAllah.

The place, where Allah ﷻ resides and

Where the RasoolAllah ﷺ will abide forever.

This place is Jannah.

Glossary

Aakhirah: Day of Judgement

Alhamdulillah: All praise and thanks be to Allah ﷻ

Aqeedah: Conviction in the Islamic faith

Bismillah: In the name of Allah ﷻ

Bi'iznillah: With the permission of Allah ﷻ

Dhikr: Remembrance of Allah ﷻ

Du'ā: Supplication/Invocation to Allah ﷻ

Dunya: This world/The present world

Emaan: Faith or belief in religious aspects of Islam

Ibadah: Worship which includes all actions done to please Allah ﷻ

Inna lillahi wa inna ilaihi rajioon: Indeed, we belong to Allah, and indeed, to Him we shall return

Islam: Peace, purity, submission and obedience to the will of Allah ﷻ

Istighfar: Seeking forgiveness from Allah ﷻ

Jannah: Paradise

Jannati: A person from paradise

Jummah: Friday

La ilaha illallah muhammadur RasoolAllah ﷺ: There is no god but Allah ﷻ, and Muhammad ﷺ is the Messenger of Allah ﷻ

Tahajjud: Voluntary prayer performed usually after waking up from sleep in the last third of the night

Qadr: Divine decree/Destiny

Qalb: Heart

Qayamah: The Day of Judgement

Qiyam Al Layl: Standing in the nigh; voluntary night prayers

Sabr: Patience

Sadaqah: Voluntary charity

Salah: The five daily prayers obligatory on every Muslim.

Salam: Peace

Shukr: Thanfulness to Allah ﷻ

SubhanAllah: Glory be to Allah ﷻ

Sujood: The act of prostration to Allah ﷻ in salah

Sunnah: Way of life, traditions; teachings, behaviours and approvals of our RasoolAllah ﷺ

Ummah: The whole community of Muslims

Wa ati'ullaha wa ati'ur'Rasool ﷺ: And obey Allah and obey RasoolAllah ﷺ

White Days: The 13th, 14th and 15th days of each lunar month in the Islamic Calender

www.ingramcontent.com/pod-product-compliance
Lightning Source LLC
Chambersburg PA
CBHW022103150726
47990CB00003B/1228